DID THE SPANISH CONQUISTADORS FIND WEALTH AND TREASURE?

BIOGRAPHY BOOK BEST SELLERS

Children's Biography Books

In this book, we're going to talk about some of the famous Spanish conquistadors. So, let's get right to it!

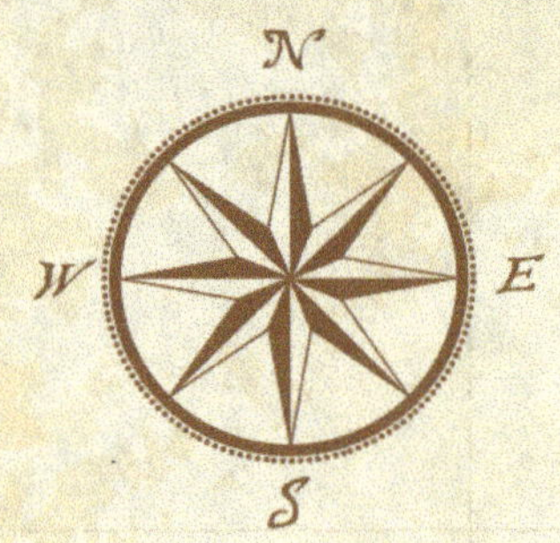

The meaning of the word "conquistador" is conqueror. The Spanish Conquistadors went forward to explore the dangerous New World and to claim lands for the kingdom of Spain. It took courage and strength to travel across the Atlantic Ocean and then explore unknown lands in North and South America.

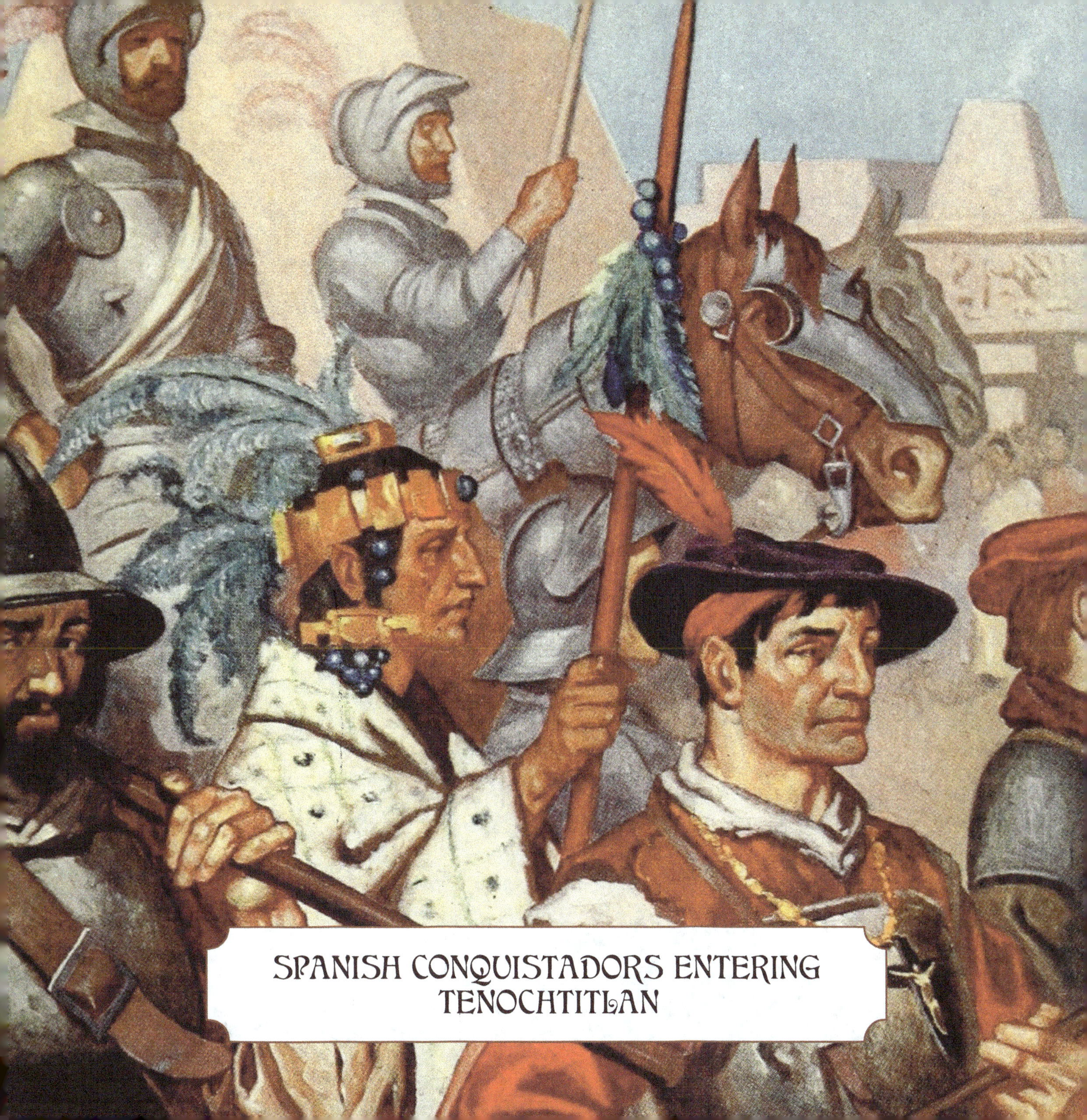

SPANISH CONQUISTADORS ENTERING
TENOCHTITLAN

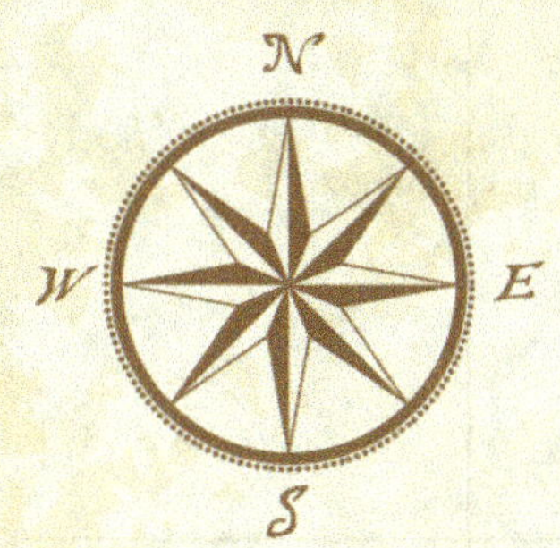

The native peoples were said to be savage. In their quest to get gold, acquire lands, and achieve fame, the Conquistadors were just as savage if not more savage than the peoples they conquered. Here are some of the most famous Spanish Conquistadors.

HERNANDO DE SOTO (1497 THROUGH 1542)

De Soto traveled with Francisco de Cordoba to explore what is now Nicaragua. Later, he was part of the Peruvian expedition led by Pizzaro. The purpose of the trip to Peru was to overthrow the Incas and obtain their gold, which they accomplished.

HERNANDO DE SOTO

KING CHARLES V

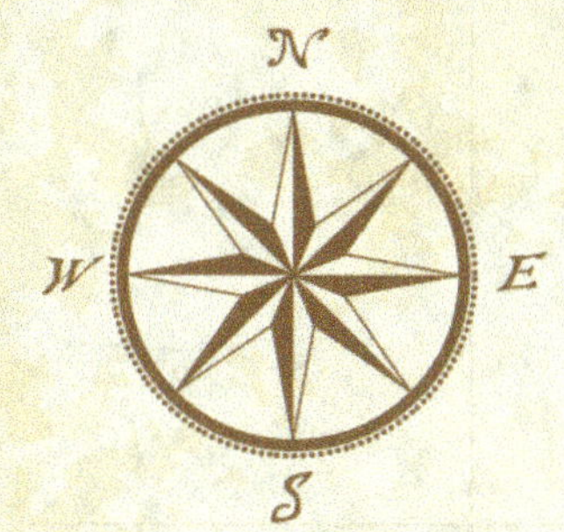

The King of Spain commissioned Hernando de Soto to lead his own expedition to explore Florida in 1539. As before, the purpose of this journey was to discover land and claim it for Spain as well as to acquire gold and other precious metals.

From South America, Hernando and his men traveled north to Florida. Then, they proceeded in a northwest direction until they came to Mabila, where there was a large fortress. Today, no one knows exactly where this fortress was, but it's believed that it was in present-day Alabama.

DE SOTO BURNS MABILA

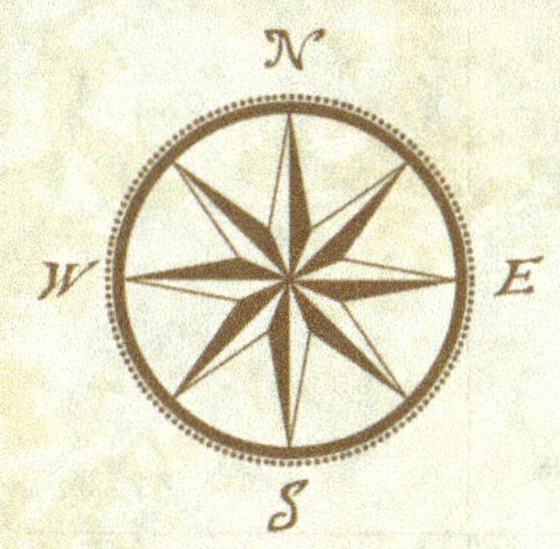

The area seemed peaceful and quiet, but when they entered, the explorer and his men were attacked. They left the city and continued the battle, but the natives fortified the gates so they couldn't get back in. In answer to this defensive strategy, Hernando de Soto and his men set the town ablaze and it burned down completely killing the 2500 natives behind the gates.

They continued to make their way inland and Hernando became the first European to cross the Mississippi and arrive on its west bank. He passed away in 1542 and his men buried him somewhere near the Mississippi River.

BURIAL OF DE SOTO

DON SEBASTIÁN DE BENALCÁZAR

SEBASTIÁN DE BELALCÁZAR (1480 THROUGH 1551)

Belalcázar escaped to the Spanish colonies to prevent punishment for a crime he had committed. He was impoverished and decided to become a conquistador to make his fortune. He joined in an alliance with conquistadors who promoted him to a position as mayor of a new settlement in the country of Nicaragua.

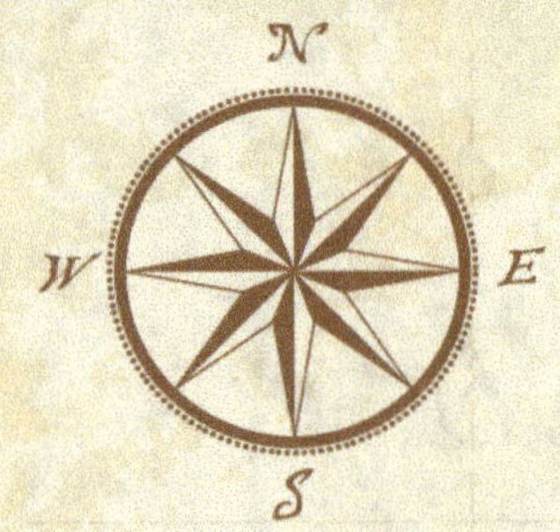

He had heard that some great treasures of gold and silver were hidden in the city of Quito, so he went there and conquered the city with no problems since there were no men around. However, he couldn't find the treasure, so he killed the women and their children as a warning of what he would do if they hid the riches from him.

MAP OF THE CITY OF QUITO

VASCO NÚÑEZ DE BALBOA (1475 THROUGH 1519)

Balboa left Spain and traveled to South America where he explored much of the coastline of the modern-day country of Columbia. For a while, he lived on the island of Hispaniola, but he went into debt as a pig farmer and had to flee to the colony of San Sebastian.

VASCO NUÑEZ DE BALBOA

BALBOA AND THE INDIAN PRINCESS

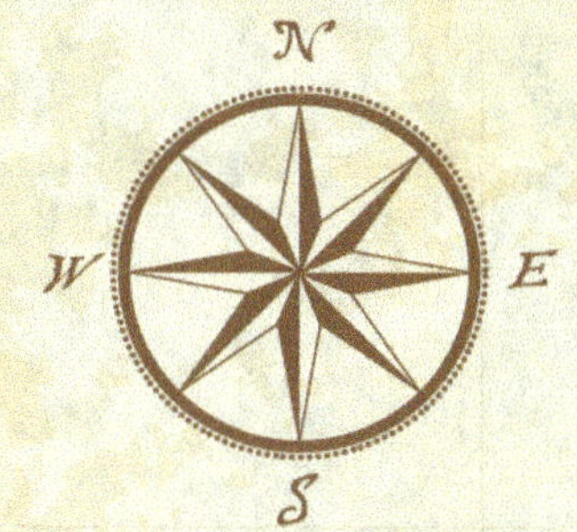

When he arrived, he discovered that many of the inhabitants had been killed by native peoples. He convinced the survivors to move to the Gulf of Uraba's west side. There, he founded the town of Darién, which was located on the small piece of land connecting Central and South America—the Isthmus of Panama. Darién was the first settlement inhabited by Europeans in South America.

QUARREL FOR THE GOLD

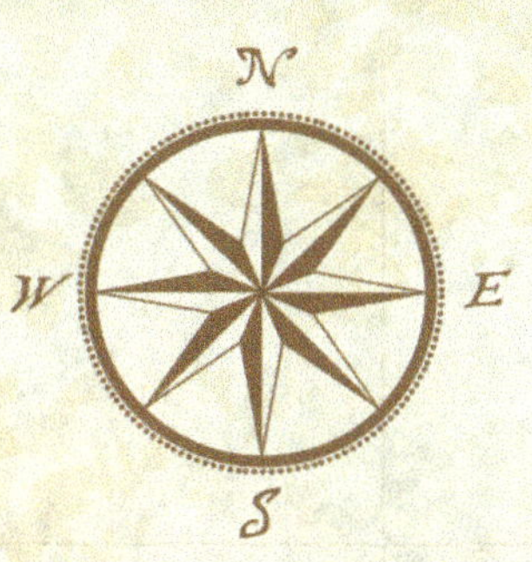

Balboa took gold from the natives and captured their people and made them slaves. His strategy was to align himself with a specific tribe or tribes and then bribe them with precious metals and slaves from their enemies. By doing this, he didn't have to defend himself and his men from all the tribes at the same time. He grabbed up their lands and expanded his territory.

I n 1513, Balboa was in charge of the first expedition that was designed to prove that the Earth was round. Despite the discovery of the New World, many people still believed that the world was flat.

The goal of their trip was to reach the coastline facing the Pacific Ocean. There was also a legend that beyond the Pacific there was a land that had even more gold than the riches of North and South America.

Balboa didn't find gold on this trip, but he claimed the beautiful Pacific coast for Spain. He was the first European to observe the Pacific Ocean from the New World. However, the king of Spain did not receive the news of Balboa's amazing discovery.

He sent a new governor called Pedro Arias de Ávila to Darién while Balboa was gone. When he returned, the new governor, who was jealous of Balboa, had him convicted of treason and had him beheaded.

DIEGO DE ALMAGRO (1475 THROUGH 1538)

Diego de Almagro only had one eye because he had lost his other eye in a fight against natives. Despite this handicap, he continued to explore South America and was the first European to get to the lands that are now the country of Chile.

DIEGO

INCA-SPANISH CONFRONTATION

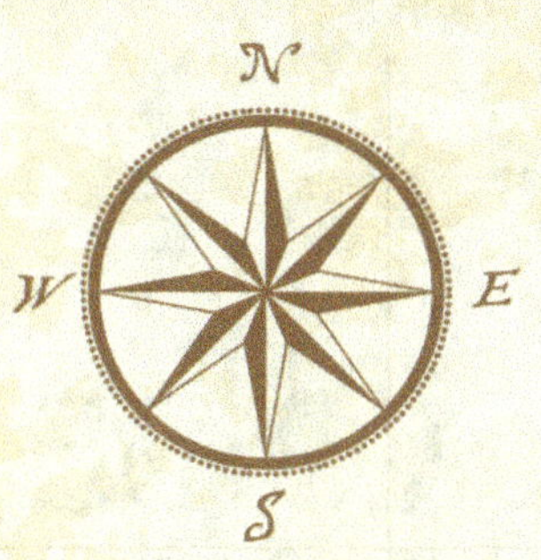

He was involved in the fighting that ended the mighty Inca Empire. The land that the conquistadors took from the Inca people became the Spanish territories in Peru. One of his enemies, another conquistador, had him executed.

FRANCISCO DE VILLAGRA (1511 THROUGH 1563)

Villagra had a plan to save Diego de Almagro from being executed, but his plan was discovered and when Diego was executed, Villagra found himself in danger. He was eventually spared by one of the Pizarro brothers.

FRANCISCO DE VILLAGRA

He participated in the overthrow and conquest of what is now the country of Chile and for his loyalty to the king he received the position of governor of the conquered country. He held the position of Chile's governor three separate times. He was a brutal leader and quickly executed those he perceived as his enemies.

FRANCISCO VÁZQUEZ DE CORONADO (1510 THROUGH 1554)

During the time of the conquistadors, there was a legend about seven cities that held incredible treasures of gold. Many conquistadors went in search of these cities and Coronado was no exception. However, he decided to look in North America instead of South America.

He traveled north from Mexico and found the Grand Canyon on his travels. He battled with the Native Americans, which was the first war between men from Europe and natives in America.

FRANCISCO PIZARRO (1478 THROUGH 1541)

Pizarro and his men destroyed the vast Inca Empire in the region of what is now the country of Peru in South America. He tried to do so unsuccessfully twice, but on his third try, with the king of Spain's approval, he was successful. He executed the Inca emperor after stealing their riches and once their leader was dead the Inca Empire fell.

FRANCISCO DE ORELLANA (1511 THROUGH 1546)

Orellana and his men were exploring the banks of the Amazon River by foot but it was dangerous and too many men were dying. They decided to sail down the river instead. This first expedition was not successful, but the second attempt was. Many of his men were killed by arrows dipped in poison that were shot by the natives in the area.

FRANCISCO DE ORELLANA

MARE OCEANUM
AFRICA
EVROPA

JUAN DE LA COSA (1460 THROUGH 1510)

The captain of one of Columbus's ships, Juan de la Cosa is known for creating the first map that displayed the Americas.

HERNAN CORTES
(1495 THROUGH 1547)

In 1519, Cortes led ships from what is now the country of Cuba to the location of the Yucatan Peninsula. Hearing that the Aztec civilization had vast amounts of treasure, Cortes traveled inland to reach the amazing capital city of Tenochtitlan. He conquered the Aztecs with help from other natives who were their enemies and killed Montezuma, their emperor.

HERNAN CORTES

DID THE CONQUISTADORS FIND THE GOLD THEY WERE SEEKING?

Many of the conquistadors did find the gold they were searching for. Disks of gold as well as masks of gold and gold jewelry were found and taken in Mexico. In Mexico's lands, there were also gold bars and gold dust and the Spaniards took those as well.

When Francisco Pizarro arrived in Peru, he demanded gold and silver to be paid as a ransom for the life of Emperor Atahualpa, leader of the Inca peoples.

The emperor filled a large room with gold, over 13,000 pounds of it, and then he filled it again with twice the amount of silver. Even though the emperor had paid the requested ransom, Pizarro killed him anyway.

MACHU PICHU

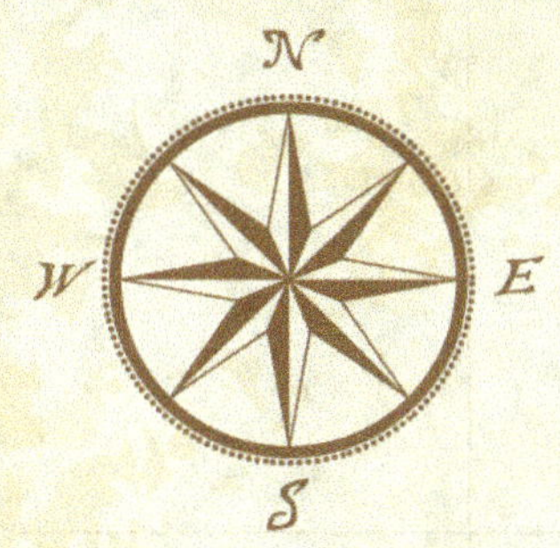

egend has it that the Spaniards didn't get all the Inca gold. A group of Atahualpa's subjects were on their way with more gold when they heard that the emperor had been killed. They supposedly hid it in a cave that wasn't marked where it was found by a Spaniard called Valverde fifty years after it was hidden. However, the treasure was lost again and found by Barth Blake in 1886. Blake died under suspicious circumstances and the treasure has never been seen again.

SUMMARY

The Spanish Conquistadors came to the New World to bravely seek treasures of gold, silver, and expansive lands that they could conquer for their kingdom.

Many of the native cultures they encountered were not afraid to shed blood to defend their civilizations, but, with their superior armor and weapons, the conquistadors brutally wiped out entire civilizations and plundered their riches.

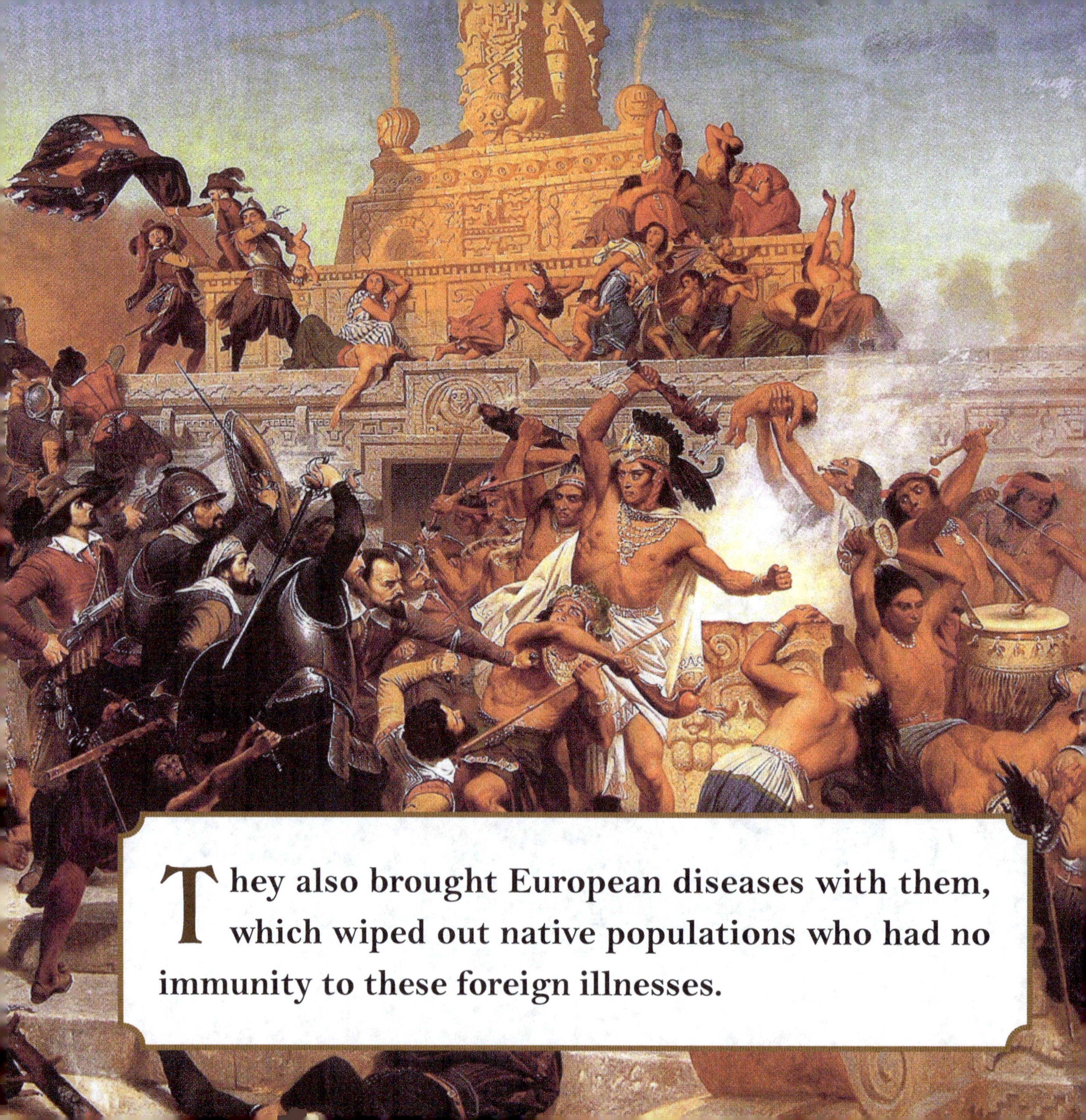

They also brought European diseases with them, which wiped out native populations who had no immunity to these foreign illnesses.

The Conquistadors frequently fought among and killed others within their group.

Now that you know more about the Spanish conquistadors, you can read about one of the civilizations they eventually overthrew in the Baby Professor book The History of the Mayan Empire.

Visit

BABY PROFESSOR
EDUCATION KIDS

www.BabyProfessorBooks.com

to download Free Baby Professor eBooks
and view our catalog of new and exciting
Children's Books